We Worship the Lord

in Simcoe County Churches

Places of worship
in Simcoe County photographed
by Eileen Murdoch
between
1986 and 2013

© Copyright 2013 Eileen Murdoch

All rights reserved. No part of this publication may be reproduced, stored in a retrieval system, or transmitted, in any form or by any means, electronic, mechanical, photocopying, recording, or otherwise, without the written prior permission of the author or copyright holder.

Editing and formatting by
Su Murdoch, City of Barrie, Ontario, Canada, L4M 4B6

The printing of *We Worship the Lord in Simcoe County Churches* is sponsored by the Barrie Historical Association.

This book is available from:

    Barrie Historical Association – or via www.barriehistorical.com
    P.O. Box 316, Barrie, Ontario, Canada, L4N 4T5

    Simcoe County Museum
    1151 Highway 26, Minesing, Ontario, Canada, L0L 1Y2

Publisher:

    The History Press, 94 Lillian Crescent, Barrie, Ontario, L4N 5H7
    www.thehistorypress.ca

Library and Archives Canada Cataloguing in Publication

Murdoch, C Eileen, 1932-, author
    We Worship the Lord in Simcoe County Churches / Eileen Murdoch.

    1. Simcoe (Ont. : County)--Church history. I. Title.

FC3095.S5M87 2014   277.13'27   C2013-908282-4

ISBN: 978-0-9808983-5-4 – Spiral Bound
          978-0-9808983-6-1 – (pbk.)

Preface

Faith, planning, financing, cooperation, labour, and prayer are involved in the building of a church. I am fascinated by the variety in architecture that congregations have used in creating their houses of worship. I am pleased to share with you my pictures of many of the churches in Simcoe County that I so admire.

Eileen Murdoch

Barrie, 2013

Introduction

The settlement of Simcoe County began in the early 19th century. The earliest settlers gathered together in a home to worship, and whenever possible, held services under the guidance of a traveling clergyman of any faith. As more families arrived, church buildings of various faiths were built. Most early churches were plain and made from local materials. As villages and towns arose and residents became more prosperous, church buildings became larger and more embellished.

With the later migration of the rural population to larger centres, churches are often the only remnant of the past life of many hamlets and crossroads communities. Some continue as places of worship, their original architecture untouched. Some have been altered, often converted to other uses. Many are abandoned or demolished with a cairn erected to mark the location.

For over twenty seven years, Eileen Murdoch has travelled throughout Simcoe County taking pictures of these landmark places of worship. Her photographs are an important record of this legacy of church buildings. Take time to appreciate their meaning and architectural glory, past and present.

Val Brucker

Vice President,
Barrie Historical Association

The photographs are arranged alphabetically by community name.

FORMAT EXPLANATION	
[NAME OF COMMUNITY] **Alliston,** [NAME OF TOWNSHIP OR TOWN] **New Tecumseth Township** [NAME OF CHURCH] Alliston Alliance [DATE OF PHOTOGRAPH] May 18, 1997 [RESEARCH DETAILS]	

Achill, Adjala-Tosorontio Township
St. Mary's Roman Catholic
May 2009

Adjala-Tosorontio Township
Raney's United
August 1999

Allenwood, Springwater Township
St. Thomas Anglican Cairn
May 26, 2003

Alliston, Town of New Tecumseth
Alliston Alliance
May 18, 1997

Alliston, Town of New Tecumseth
Alliston Christian Fellowship
January 28, 2002

Alliston, Town of New Tecumseth
Alliston Christian Reformed
August 2013

A

Alliston, Town of New Tecumseth
Alliston Pentecostal
August 2013

Alliston, Town of New Tecumseth
Grace Baptist
July 25, 2005

Alliston, Town of New Tecumseth
Knox Presbyterian
2013

Alliston, Town of New Tecumseth
St. Andrew's Anglican
August 2013

Alliston, Town of New Tecumseth
St. John's United
August 2013

When opened in 1872, this church had a brick tower and wood spire measuring 130 feet in height. In January 1949, a windstorm broke the spire off at the junction of the wood and brick, tumbling it to the ground. Repairs were made to the brickwork and a roof was constructed over the tower, but the spire was not replaced. In 2002, a new spire was installed.

Alliston, Town of New Tecumseth
St. Paul's the Apostle Roman Catholic
September 16, 1997

Angus, Essa Township
Angus United
May 11, 2005

During the First World War when there were 50,000 troops based at Camp Borden, reading rooms, lounges, and meetings were provided every night for the soldiers. In 1954, the minister inducted was the first female minister in the Simcoe County United Church Presbytery.

Angus, Essa Township
Living Hope Fellowship
August 2013

Angus, Essa Township
Our Lady of Grace Roman Catholic
July 8, 2013

Angus, Essa Township
Pinewoods Gospel Chapel (former)
September 1999

Angus, Essa Township
Zion Presbyterian

Anten Mills, Springwater Township
Anten Mills United (closed)
1997
In 1940, a man planted five blue spruce trees in the churchyard in honour of his five sisters.

Ardtrea, Severn Township
Ardtrea United
This was dedicated as a Methodist church in September 1888.

Arlington, Adjala-Tosorontio Township
Immaculate Conception Roman Catholic
September 2013

Atherley, Ramara Township
Atherley United
The steeple was blown off in a hurricane in 1908 and later replaced with a smaller steeple.

Atherley, Ramara Township
Seventh Day Adventist and Church of Good Shepherd Reformed Episcopal
June 7, 2000

Avening, Clearview Township
Avening United
August 2013

Banda, Clearview Township
Christ Church Anglican (closed)
April 3, 2001
When built in 1865, the building proved too large to heat so in 1897, it was rebuilt smaller.

Barrie, City of
Barrie Alliance (former)
August 17, 2000

Barrie, City of
Barrie Free Methodist (former)
September 1999

Barrie, City of
Barrie Free Methodist
August 20, 2004

Barrie, City of
Barrie Free Presbyterian

Barrie, City of
Barrie Seventh Day Adventist (former)
(former Holly United)
September 1999

Barrie, City of
Barrie Seventh Day Adventist
August 2013

Barrie, City of
Bethel Community (former)
May 17, 2002

Barrie, City of
Bethel Community
2007

Barrie, City of
Burton Avenue United
July 4, 2005

When built in 1873, the lumber cost six dollars per thousand board feet. The name Allandale Methodist Church was changed to Burton Avenue Methodist Church in May 1896.

Barrie, City of
Central United
April 9, 2004

When Hurricane Hazel hit Barrie in October 1954, floods undermined the foundation of the church building at the corner of Toronto Street and Elizabeth Street (now Dunlop Street West). The congregation then built this structure at the corner of Toronto and Ross streets.

Barrie, City of
Church of Christ
June 25, 2002

Barrie, City of
Church of Jesus Christ of the Latter Day Saints
May 1997

Barrie, City of
Collier Street United
June 2009

When the new bell rang for the first time in 1873 to call to worship, the newspaper reported that people were rushing around wondering where there was a fire.

Both grandfathers and an uncle of Canadian Prime Minister Lester B. Pearson were ministers here at different dates. Mr. A.F.A. Malcolmson was a Sunday School teacher there for fifty three years.

Barrie, City of
Community of Christ (former; demolished)
(Reorganized Church of Jesus Christ of the Latter Day Saints)   February 27, 1999

Barrie, City of
Covenant Christian Reformed
December 28, 1998

Barrie, City of
Emmanuel Baptist (former)

Barrie, City of
Emmanuel Baptist
October 7, 2005

Barrie, City of
Essa Road Presbyterian   1996
The congregation paid $260 for the land on which this church is located.

Barrie, City of
Exaltation of the Holy Cross Ukrainian Catholic

Barrie, City of
First Baptist (former)   October 1996
In the early days, members were disciplined if they missed more than three consecutive services without a good reason.

Barrie, City of
First Baptist
December 19, 2006
In 1982 the property for a new church was bought for $60,000 but it was not built until 1997.

Barrie, City of
First Christian Reformed (former)
August 17, 2002

Barrie, City of
First Christian Reformed
June 2012

Barrie, City of
Full Gospel Lighthouse
1995

Barrie, City of
Gospel Hall (former)
January 8, 2000

Barrie, City of
Grace United
April 14, 2001

Barrie, City of
Heritage Baptist
December 28, 1998

Barrie, City of
Hi-Way Pentecostal
September 1999

Barrie, City of
Holy Spirit Roman Catholic
August 2013

B

Barrie, City of
Inniswood Baptist (former)
September 1999

Barrie, City of
Inniswood Baptist

Barrie, City of
Loving Saviour Lutheran
May 26, 2004

Barrie, City of
Lutheran Church of the Good Shepherd
October 2011
Built in 1959, this is an outreach of Holy Trinity Lutheran in Bradford.

Barrie, City of
Maple Grove Community (former Church of the Nazarene) (closed)   May 1997

Barrie, City of
Mapleview Community
December 2011

We Worship the Lord in Simcoe County Churches

Barrie, City of
New Apostolic
2013

Barrie, City of
Northside Bible Chapel
May 1997

Barrie, City of
Northwest Barrie United
December 27, 2002

Barrie, City of
Oasis of Hope (former Mapleview Community)
October 1999

Barrie, City of
St. Andrew's Presbyterian
June 2012

In July 1883, the wooden sidewalk on Owen Street between Collier Street and St. Andrew's was completed. The planks were laid lengthwise.

Barrie, City of
St. George's Anglican

When the cornerstone for this Allandale, now Barrie, church was laid in 1891, the congregation and clergy marched from their meeting hall to the new site singing "The Church's One Foundation." The bell was hung in 1896 and weighs 639 pounds.

Barrie, City of
St. Giles Anglican
May 12, 2012

Barrie, City of
St. John Vianney Roman Catholic
February 27, 1999

Barrie, City of
St. Margaret's Anglican
September 2011

Barrie, City of
St. Mary's Roman Catholic
August 2013

In 1926, dynamite was put in the brick wall of the furnace room of the former St. Mary's church on Mulcaster Street. When it blew, it did a lot of damage but did not destroy the building. The man responsible was caught and he admitted having had orders from the Ku Klux Klan to blow up the church. This new church was later built on Amelia Street.

Barrie, City of
Salvation Army Citadel
September 1999

Barrie, City of
Trinity Anglican
September 25, 1999

When opened in 1864, the spire was 131 feet tall. It was struck by lightning in 1934 and the interior destroyed. The interior was rebuilt the same year but the spire was never reconstructed.

The minister announced in 1908 that during July and August he would preach ten minute sermons.

Barrie, City of
Westminster Presbyterian

Barrie, City of
Westside Evangelical Lutheran
August 3, 2004

Base Borden, Essa Township
St. Joseph's Roman Catholic Chapel
July 24, 2000

Base Borden, Essa Township
Trinity Protestant Chapel
July 24, 2000

Batteaux, Clearview Township
Christ Church Anglican
September 1999

In 1916, lightning struck the side of the church creating a hole and reducing the pews and furnishings inside to fragments.

Baxter, Essa Township
Lighthouse Baptist (former Baxter Presbyterian)
April 2006
Electric lights were installed in 1952.

Baxter, Essa Township
Living Faith Community Presbyterian
August 2013

Beeton, Town of New Tecumseth
St. Andrew's Presbyterian
March 25, 2003

In 1879, about forty of the church members voted in favour, and about twenty voted against, installing an organ.

Beeton, Town of New Tecumseth
St. Paul's Anglican (closed)
2001

Beeton, Town of New Tecumseth
Trinity United
May 25, 2005

The minister in 1926 had a weak voice so a large umbrella was placed behind the pulpit to carry the sound of his voice out to the congregation.

Bell Ewart, Town of Innisfil
Bell Ewart Community Baptist
December 15, 1998

The Tollendal Baptist church building was moved across the ice on Lake Simcoe to become the Bell Ewart Baptist church.

Bell Ewart, Town of Innisfil
Church of Assumption of Our Lady
Roman Catholic (closed)
December 14, 1998

Black River, Ramara Township
St. Joseph's Roman Catholic
June 1, 2006

Bond Head, Town of Bradford-West Gwillimbury
Bond Head United
October 1999

Bond Head, Town of Bradford-West Gwillimbury
Trinity Anglican (former)
(now St. Catherine of Alexandria Catholic)
November 21, 2006

Bond Head, Town of Bradford-West Gwillimbury St. Catherine of Alexandria Catholic (former Trinity Anglican) 2011

Bradford, Town of Bradford-West Gwillimbury
Bradford Alliance
May 2, 2006

Bradford,
Town of Bradford-West Gwillimbury
Bradford Baptist
September 2013

Bradford,
Town of Bradford-West Gwillimbury
Bradford Pentecostal Community
May 2, 2006

Bradford,
Town of Bradford-West Gwillimbury
Bradford United
November 1999

Bradford,
Town of Bradford-West Gwillimbury
Holy Martyrs of Japan Roman Catholic
February 27, 1999

This church is dedicated to the memory of six missionaries and twenty native Japanese who were put to death in Japan by being bound to crosses and then pierced with spears.

**Bradford,
Town of Bradford-West Gwillimbury**
Holy Trinity Lutheran
February 29, 2000

When this church opened in 1957, there were three worship services: one in Slovak, one in English, and one in German.

**Bradford,
Town of Bradford-West Gwillimbury**
St. John's Presbyterian (former)
1999

Bradford, Town of Bradford-West Gwillimbury
St. John's Presbyterian   May 2, 2006

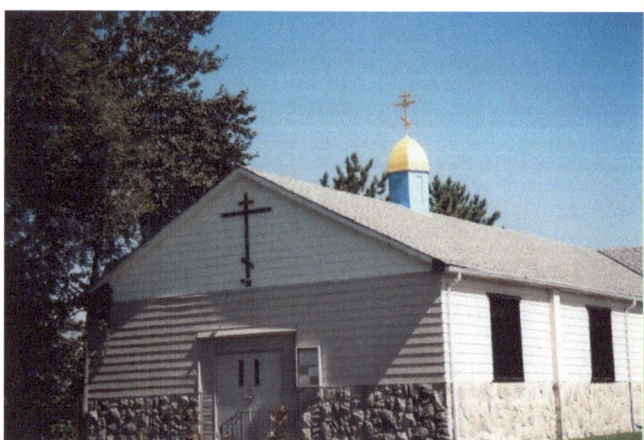

Bradford, Town of Bradford-West Gwillimbury
St. Michael's Orthodox   September 2013

**Bradford,
Town of Bradford-West Gwillimbury**
Trinity Anglican
May 2, 2006

Bradford-West Gwillimbury, Town of
Scotch Settlement Presbyterian
September 2013

Bradford-West Gwillimbury, Town of
Auld Kirk
February 29, 2000

This was built by Scottish settlers who left Scotland when landowners got rid of crofters (individual farmers) to establish sheep farms. Lord Selkirk took many to settle in the Red River area of Manitoba. Some left by canoe and travelled to West Gwillimbury Township. Auld Kirk is on the Sixth Line. It has not been used for many years.

Brechin, Ramara Township
Brechin United
May 1997

Brechin, Ramara Township
St. Andrew's Roman Catholic
May 1997

Brentwood, Clearview Township
Our Lady of Assumption Roman Catholic
July 26, 2013

Cawaja Beach, Tiny Township
St. Volodymyr and Olha Ukrainian Orthodox
1996

Churchill, Town of Innisfil
Churchill United
October 1996

Churchill, Town of Innisfil
St. Peter's Anglican
2011

Clearview Township
Church of the Messiah Anglican (former)
May 17, 2000

Clearview Township
Clearview Methodist cairn (Sunnidale Township)
2000

C

Clearview Township
East Nottawasaga Presbyterian (former)
September 5, 1997

This was built in 1854 and bricked in 1881. It is on the road north of Creemore.

Clearview Township
Emmanuel Presbyterian September 5, 1997

Clearview Township
West Nottawasaga Presbyterian (former)
March 2000

Clougher, Adjala-Tosorontio Township
St. James Anglican
August 2013

At Airlie (now called Clougher) there was a church on each of the three corners of an intersection: Methodist, Presbyterian (opened in January 1890), and Anglican. The Methodist Church is gone; the Presbyterian Church became the parish hall of St. James Anglican.

Clougher, Adjala-Tosorontio Township
St. James Anglican Parish Hall
July 26, 2013

This is the parish hall, formerly the Calvin Presbyterian church building.

Coldwater, Severn Township
Coldwater United
October 5, 2005

Coldwater, Severn Township
St. Andrew's Presbyterian
April 1, 1997

Coldwater, Severn Township
St. Mathias Anglican

Colgan, Adjala-Tosorontio Township
St. James' Roman Catholic

Collingwood, Town of
All Saints Anglican
August 2013

Collingwood, Town of
Christ Our Hope Lutheran
September 1999

Collingwood, Town of
Christian Reformed
September 1999
From its establishment in 1953 until 1966, all services were conducted in Dutch.

Collingwood, Town of
Church of Christ
August 2013

Collingwood, Town of
Church of God of Prophesy
September 1999

Collingwood, Town of
Church of Nazarene
September 1999

Collingwood, Town of
Collingwood Evangelical Missionary
August 2013

Collingwood, Town of
Fellowship Baptist
August 2013

Collingwood, Town of
First Baptist
August 2013

One evening in December 1878, an attempt was made to burn the church. A quantity of rags saturated with oil and set on fire were stuffed through a window broken at the back of the building. The caretaker discovered the still smoldering rags and saved the church.

Collingwood, Town of
First Presbyterian
August 2013

In early days, the minister was given a gift of a Persian lamb coat and cap with several gold pieces in the pocket.

Collingwood, Town of
Gospel Hall
September 30, 2006

Collingwood, Town of
Heritage Community
August 2013

Collingwood, Town of
New Life Brethren in Christ
August 2013

Collingwood, Town of
Reorganized Church of Jesus Christ
of the Latter Day Saints
September 1999

Collingwood, Town of
St. Mary's Roman Catholic
August 2013

Collingwood, Town of
Salvation Army Citadel
August 2013

Collingwood, Town of
Trinity United
August 2013

Cookstown, Town of Innisfil
Cookstown Presbyterian (former)
November 28, 2001

Cookstown, Town of Innisfil
Cookstown United
November 28, 2001

Cookstown, Town of Innisfil
Laestadian Lutheran
May 19, 2004

Cookstown, Town of Innisfil
St. John's Anglican
May 3, 2005

Coulson, Oro-Medonte Township
Coulson United (former)
September 1995

Coulson's Hill, Town of Bradford-West Gwillimbury
St. John's Presbyterian (former)
August 12, 2013

C

We Worship the Lord in Simcoe County Churches | 35

Coulson's Hill, Town of Bradford-West Gwillimbury
St. Paul's Anglican
August 12, 2013

Craighurst, Oro-Medonte Township
Knox Presbyterian
2011

John Knox was a Scottish clergyman and leader of the Protestant Reformation. He is considered the founder of the Presbyterian denomination in Scotland. There are at least eight Knox Presbyterian churches in Simcoe County.

Craighurst, Oro-Medonte Township
St. John's Anglican
2009

Creemore, Clearview Township
Creemore Baptist
December 15, 1998

Creemore, Clearview Township
St. Andrew's Presbyterian
May 17, 2000

In 1863, this was part of a four point charge. The minister travelled by horseback with a horse and saddle provided by the congregation.

Creemore, Clearview Township
St. John's United
August 2013

The first time the bells at St. John's (then Methodist) were used was to ring out the old year 1899 and ring in the new year 1900.

Creemore, Clearview Township
St. Luke's Anglican
April 24, 2003

When opened, friends of the rector in England donated the stained glass windows in the chancel.

Crossland, Springwater Township
Knox Flos Presbyterian
2005   The congregation decided in 1898 to sing "Amen" only after the last hymn of the service.

Crown Hill, Oro-Medonte Township
Crown Hill United
May 25, 2013

Crown Hill, Springwater Township
Holy Cross Greek Orthodox
October 25, 2006

This building was St. James' Anglican.

Cumberland Beach, Severn Township
Hope Community Christian
September 4, 2013

Dalston, Springwater Township
Dalston United
1995

Dunedin, Clearview Township
Knox Presbyterian
September 5, 1997

Dunkerron, Town of Bradford-West Gwillimbury
Dunkerron United (closed)
June 16, 1999

Duntroon, Clearview Township
Anglican Church of the Redeemer
September 1999

Duntroon, Clearview Township
St. Paul's Presbyterian (former)
March 1997

Eady, Oro-Medonte Township
Wesley United
August 2011

East Oro, Oro-Medonte Township
St. Mark's Anglican (former) This was built in 1880, closed in 1969, and demolished in 1987 just before this photograph was taken.

Ebenezer, Tay Township
Ebenezer United
July 24, 2013

Edenvale, Springwater Township
Edenvale United cairn

Edgar, Oro-Medonte Township
African Methodist Episcopal
2012

This log church near Edgar was built about 1849 by Black settlers in Oro Township. Only a few descendants remain in the area. Occasionally, a worship service is held and attended by descendants, Afro Canadians, and local people.

Edgar, Oro-Medonte Township
Edgar United cairn
August 18, 2001

Edgar, Oro-Medonte Township
West Oro Baptist
2010

Elmgrove, Essa Township
St. Peter's Anglican cairn

Elmvale, Springwater Township
Elmvale Community
June 5, 1998

Elmvale, Springwater Township
Elmvale Presbyterian
May 11, 2009

For several years, the bell at this church was used as the village fire alarm.

Elmvale, Springwater Township
Our Lady of Lourdes Roman Catholic
March 16, 1998

Elmvale, Springwater Township
St. John's United
March 16, 1998

When it was decided in 1974 to renovate the sanctuary, the congregation agreed to send the same amount of money spent on the renovations to World Development.

Elmvale, Springwater Township
Wycliffe Anglican
March 16, 1998

Essa Township
Burns United cairn
October 2000

Essa Township
Essa Townline Presbyterian (former)
April 22, 2013

Everett, Adjala-Tosorontio Township
St. David's Anglican
August 2013

When this church opened in July 1880, they had three services on that day. People brought their picnic baskets and stayed all day. It was estimated that 1,500 attended.

Fairvalley, Oro-Medonte Township
St. George's Anglican
April 20, 2003

This church was founded in 1832 when the Captain Elmes Steele family, famous for Sir Sam Steele of the North West Mounted Police, donated four acres of their land for a church and cemetery. The current church building was erected in 1884.

Fergusonvale, Springwater Township
Presbyterian (former)
May 17, 2000

Fesserton, Severn Township
Gospel Lighthouse
October 8, 2001

Forest Home, Oro-Medonte Township
Forest Home United
November 2011

Gamebridge, Ramara Township
Knox Presbyterian
June 1, 2006

Gilford, Town of Innisfil
Gilford United
April 21, 2003

Glencairn, Adjala-Tosorontio Township
Church of the Disciples of Christ (former)

G

Glencairn, Adjala-Tosorontio Township
Hope Acres Salvation Army
August 2002

Glen Huron, Clearview Township
Glen Huron Memorial Anglican Chapel (closed)
June 19, 2002

The Anglicans residing in the Glen Huron area held services in the Orange Hall for fifty years before building a church in 1953-54.

Glen Huron, Clearview Township
Glen Huron United
March 28, 2000

Grenfel, Springwater Township
Grenfel United
August 2013

Guthrie, Oro-Medonte Township
Guthrie Presbyterian (former)

This was built in 1927 by those members of the Guthrie Presbyterian congregation who did not agree with the United Church union in 1925.

Guthrie, Oro-Medonte Township
Guthrie United (former)
October 22, 1991

This was Presbyterian until the United Church union in 1925. Before they had their own church, some Scottish folk walked about nine miles to worship at Knox Presbyterian at the corner of 9th Line and Old Barrie Road.

In 1888, the minister wanted the congregation to stand to sing and sit to pray. This was opposite to what had been done. Some were so upset with this idea that they left the congregation. In the 1890s, there was a canvass to raise money for two pulpit Bibles: one in English and one in Gaelic.

Hamlet, Severn Township
St. Luke's Anglican (former)

About 1875, timber for building this church was cut not far from the site. It was taken to Christie's Mill at Severn Bridge, made into planks, floated as a raft and towed down the Severn River by steamboat, dragged ashore, and drawn by carts to the building site.

Hamlet, Severn Township
St. Luke's Anglican cairn
June 2000

Hampshire Mills, Severn Township
Christian Fellowship Chapel
2001

Hawkestone, Oro-Medonte Township
Hawkestone United (former)
February 7, 2005

In May 1896, the cornerstone was laid for the new Methodist (now United) church.

Hawkestone, Oro-Medonte Township
St. Aiden's Anglican (former)
November 2002

Hillsdale, Springwater Township
St. Andrew's Presbyterian

Work began in July 1896 on this $5,000 building. When the Reverend Neil Campbell of Oro attended the laying of the cornerstone, he declared, "Grace, gumption, grit, and greenbacks were necessary factors in a prosperous congregation!"

Hillsdale, Springwater Township
Hillsdale United (former)
May 2000

Hobart, Oro-Medonte Township
Hobart Memorial (former)

This church was dedicated in 1835.

Hockley, Adjala-Tosorontio Township
St. James Anglican (closed)
August 1999

Holland Marsh, Town of Bradford-West Gwillimbury
Springdale Christian Reformed
August 16, 2000

Horseshoe Valley, Oro-Medonte Township
Ellsmere Chapel

The chapel at Horseshoe Valley Ski Resort is named for the family that settled on the land in the 1830s.

Innisfil, Town of
Innisfil Community Pentecostal

Innisfil, Town of
New Life Baptist
2011

Innisfil, Town of
New Life Baptist
May 7, 2013
Building the new church.

Ivy, Essa Township
Christ Church St. Jude's Anglican
April 8, 2013

We Worship the Lord in Simcoe County Churches | 49

Ivy, Essa Township
Ivy Presbyterian
July 27, 2005

In 1903: "The Presbyterians gave their minister a pleasant surprise by presenting him with 40 bushels of oats."

Jack's Lake, Springwater Township
Ebenezer United Missionary (former)
September 5, 1997

Jarratt, Oro-Medonte Township
Willis Presbyterian
October 1, 2001

The church is named for Michael Willis, a principal and professor at Knox College, University of Toronto.

Lafontaine, Tiny Township
Lafontaine – St. Croix Roman Catholic
(Paroisse Sainte Croix)
June 1996

This church is a distance back from the street because it was built behind the older church. The congregation worshipped in one while the other was under construction. The steeple is 120 feet tall.

Lavender, Clearview Township
Lavender United (former)
August 3, 2002

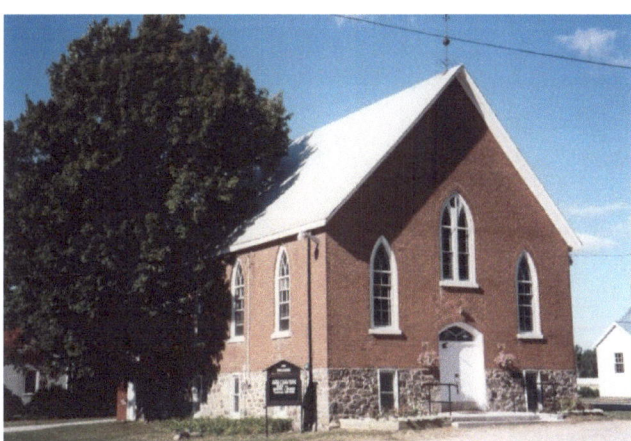

Lefroy, Town of Innisfil
Lefroy United
September 1999

Longford Mills, Ramara Township
Longford Mills Anglican (former)
October 26, 2001

Longford Mills, Ramara Township
Longford Mills United (former)
May 1997

Marchmont, Severn Township
Marchmont Baptist
August 2011

Midhurst (Simcoe County Museum), Springwater Township
Vespra Christ Church Anglican
October 2000   This was moved to the Museum.

Midhurst, Springwater Township
Midhurst United
July 24, 2002

Midhurst, Springwater Township
St. Paul's Anglican (former)

Midhurst, Springwater Township
St. Paul's Anglican
2007

Midhurst, Springwater Township
Willow Creek Baptist
October 18, 2001

Midland, Town of
Calvary Baptist
February 21, 1999

Midland, Town of
Church of the Latter Day Saints
September 2013

Midland, Town of
Gospel Hall
February 21, 1999

Midland, Town of
Holy Cross Evangelical Lutheran (former)
September 1999

Midland, Town of
Knox Presbyterian
June 2012

Midland, Town of
Martyrs' Shrine
1995

When Martyrs' Shrine was dedicated in 1926, about 5,000 attended on Saturday and 10,000 on Sunday. The stone used in the building is from the Longford Mills quarry in Rama Township. The Pope visited the Shrine in 1984.

Midland, Town of
Midland Alliance
February 21, 1999

Midland, Town of
Midland Pentecostal
November 19, 1999

Midland, Town of
River of Life
September 2013

Midland, Town of
St. Margaret's Roman Catholic
July 24, 2013

The bells were installed in 1922 in memory of soldiers who lost their lives in the First World War.

Midland, Town of
St. Mark's Anglican
September 29, 2006

Midland, Town of
Salvation Army
February 21, 1999

Midland, Town of
St. Paul's United
September 29, 2006

Minesing, Springwater Township
Minesing United

Minesing, Springwater Township
St. Peter's Anglican (closed)
August 2013

In the early days, the Anglicans in Minesing rented the Temperance Hall for their worship services, paying twenty five cents per week rental.

Mitchell Square, Oro-Medonte Township
Mitchell Square Baptist (former)

Moonstone, Oro-Medonte Township
Knox Presbyterian (former)

Mount St. Louis, Oro-Medonte Township
Mount St. Louis Roman Catholic
May 2013

When St. Mary's Roman Catholic at Vigo opened in 1870, each family had a hitching post with a hole bored near the top for the reins of the horses. When the church closed, the lumber was used to build the rectory at Mount St. Louis.

New Lowell, Clearview Township
New Lowell United
July 24, 2002

New Tecumseth, Town of
St. John's Anglican
2011

Newton Robinson, Town of Bradford West-Gwillimbury
Newton Robinson United
2011

In 1890: "'We glory in tribulation' was the subject of the discourse by the Reverend at Newton Robinson, the other Sunday. How many really do glory in tribulation has not been lately enumerated."

In January 1935: "The menfolk of the United Church held a very successful wood 'bee' cutting more than thirty cords in Walter McLean's wood lot."

North River, Severn Township
St. John's Matchedash Anglican
August 1999

Nottawa, Clearview Township
Cornerstone Pentecostal
August 2013

Nottawa, Clearview Township
Nottawa Presbyterian (former)
August 2013

Nottawa, Clearview Township
Nottawa United
August 2013

The Methodists built this church and opened for divine services on August 27, 1869.

Orillia, City of
Bethel Baptist
July 5, 2005

Orillia, City of
Calvary Pentecostal Tabernacle
August 2013

Orillia, City of
Christian Reformed
August 2013

Orillia, City of
Church of Jesus Christ of the Latter Day Saints
December 10, 1998

Orillia, City of
Church on the Hill
August 2013

Orillia, City of
Covenant Reformed Baptist
July 4, 2005

Orillia, City of
Dominion Gospel Hall Assembly
August 17, 1997

Orillia, City of
First Baptist
2006

Orillia, City of
Guardian Angels Roman Catholic

The bell was installed in 1933. It weighs 2,451 pounds and has a diameter of four feet. The cross at the top of the spire stands 264 feet above the ground. The church is on a hill so when the cross is lit up at night it can be seen for a long distance.

Orillia, City of
Hillside Bible Chapel
April 2006

Orillia, City of
Holy Canadian Martyrs Roman Catholic
August 2013

Orillia, City of
Karen Crescent Free Methodist (former)
August 9, 1997

Orillia, City of
New Apostolic Wyndotte Street
August 27, 2001

Orillia, City of
North Country Baptist
July 5, 2013

Orillia, City of
Orillia Alliance
2009

Orillia, City of
Orillia Presbyterian (St. Andrew's)
May 1997

About 1865 when an organ was introduced, some were so opposed that they carried it out of the church. When it was pointed out that the Scriptures talk about the harp being a part of worship, they agreed to allow the organ.

Orillia, City of
Regent Park United
April 2006

Orillia, City of
St. Athanasius Anglican and (former) Holy Cross Lutheran   August 1997
This is an outreach of St. James' Anglican.

Orillia, City of
St. David's Anglican and Lutheran
August 2013

The mayor of Orillia donated three lots at the corner of Regent and James streets and $500 toward construction of this church. It opened in 1913. Wood for heating was cut when the men of the congregation held a "bee" on New Year's Day. They cut wood at Victoria Point, hauled it to the church as poles, and later cut it into stove size lengths.

A wood sidewalk was built along James Street, ending at the church. There was a large hedge on the corner of the property. People would walk as far as the church, leave their overshoes on a bush, and go on the dry sidewalk to downtown. They collected their overshoes on their way home.

Orillia, City of
St. James Anglican
August 17, 1997

In April 1907, the windows were taken out of the church to make way for the memorial windows. The old windows were donated for use in a church to be erected in Hawkestone.

Orillia, City of
St. Mark's Presbyterian
October 23, 2006
This is an outreach of Orillia Presbyterian.

Orillia, City of
St. Paul's United
December 28, 1996

Orillia, City of
Salvation Army Citadel
August 17, 1997

Orillia, City of
Simcoeside Lifepoint Chapel
August 1997

This is an outreach of West Street Gospel Hall (Hillside Bible Chapel). It was formerly known as Simcoeside Bible Chapel.

Orillia, City of
Westmount United
July 5, 2005

Westmount is an outreach of St. Paul's United. When Uhthoff United closed in 1968, a cross handcrafted by a local man was mounted at the front of the sanctuary. It was returned to him and he donated it to Warminster United. When that church closed, it was given to Westmount United.

Oro-Medonte Township
Calvary Community Pentecostal (Oakland Hill)
May 16, 2013

Oro-Medonte Township
Clowes Primitive Methodist cairn
2010

Oro-Medonte Township
Grace United Reformed
May 27, 1997

The building was Central Oro Presbyterian.

The Reverend Neil Campbell received $800 salary when he became pastor of a charge with three Presbyterian churches. Nineteen years later, his salary was unchanged.

Oro-Medonte Township
Knox Presbyterian (former)
September 2012
The timbers for the church were cut on site.

Oro-Medonte Township
(Old) West Oro Baptist (former)
May 17, 2013

Oro Station, Oro-Medonte Township
Oro Station United (former)
May 2010

Oro Station, Oro-Medonte Township
St. Andrew's Presbyterian (former)
2000

Oro Station, Oro-Medonte Township
St. John the Baptist St. Elizabeth Egyptian Coptic Orthodox
May 23, 2012

Oro Station, Oro-Medonte Township
Trinity Community Presbyterian
May 2012

When built, there were no stained glass windows, no altar, no hymn books, and no cross in the sanctuary. Instead, the four hundred seat auditorium was dominated by a huge screen for audio visual presentations and an orchestra for contemporary music. They claimed no change in the fundamental message, just a change in form.

Penetanguishene, Tiny Township
All Saints Anglican

In 1878, the president of the North Simcoe railway, Mr. McMurray, presented the church with a large bell.

Penetanguishene, Tiny Township
Covenant Christian Community Brethren in Christ

Penetanguishene, Tiny Township
First Presbyterian
May 3, 2006

Penetanguishene, Tiny Township
Our Lady of the Rosary Roman Catholic
March 2000

Penetanguishene, Tiny Township
St. Ann's Roman Catholic
June 2010

When the cornerstone was laid, about 4,000 attended. A special train came from Barrie with 600 on board. Steamers brought others from Parry Sound, Waubaushene, Victoria Harbour, Port Severn, Collingwood, and as far north as the French River. It was sixteen years before the building was completed in 1902 and ninety seven years in 1999, before the two spires were installed. The church has three main bells and one smaller bell weighing 1,500, 800, and 475 pounds each. The smallest is from the first St. Ann's and used in a second building before being placed in the existing church. It is from a schooner believed to be either the *Tigress* or *Scorpion*. When the bells were consecrated in January 1909, an ancient European custom meant each villager had a turn at ringing the bells.

Penetanguishene, Tiny Township
St. James-on-the-Lines Anglican

This historic church was built between 1836 and 1840 to serve the naval and military garrison and the town of Penetanguishene. It is located halfway between the two on what was considered the "line" of communication between the garrison and York (Toronto). The centre aisle is wide enough for soldiers to march four abreast.

Perkinsfield, Tiny Township
St. Patrick's Roman Catholic
July 2011

Phelpston, Springwater Township
St. Patrick's Roman Catholic
May 2010

When built in 1893, this large church cost $13,925.77. A bronze bell made in France was installed in 1926. At the dedication ceremony, the bell was decorated with flowers. In 1997, fire destroyed all but the floor and exterior brick. A lack of water made it difficult for firefighters to hold back the flames. It took two years to restore the building.

Pinkerton, Town of Bradford-West Gwillimbury
Anglican Church of St. Luke (closed)

Port McNicoll, Tay Township
Bonar Presbyterian

The church held a Mariners Service at the beginning of every sailing season, to remember God, to remember those lost at sea, and to pray for the safety of all sailors.

Port McNicoll, Tay Township
Sacred Heart Roman Catholic
July 30, 2002

Port Severn, Severn Township
St. John Baptist Roman Catholic
August 1999

Port Stanton, Severn Township
Church of Good Shepherd
October 2001

Price's Corners, Oro-Medonte Township
St. Luke's Anglican
August 2011

Ramara Township
Full Gospel Church of the Deliverance
August 2001

Ramara Township
Rama United
September 1999

Rich Hill, Town of New Tecumseth
Rich Hill United
May 25, 2005

The wind toppled the steeple on this church in 1928. It was not replaced until August 2001.

Rosemont, Town of New Tecumseth
Trinity Centennial United

Rugby, Oro-Medonte Township
Esson Presbyterian
2011

This was named for Henry Esson, a professor at Knox College, University of Toronto.

St. Paul's, Town of Innisfil
St. Paul's Anglican
June 2009

When St. Paul's opened in 1875, Canada's first prime minister, John A. Macdonald, was part of the congregation. He was not in office at that time as his terms were 1867 to 1873 and 1878 to 1891.

Senator G.W. Allan was a loyal supporter of this church. His daughter's father-in-law was a Canon in England and donated a bell for St. Paul's while visiting Canada. It is said that the train stopped at St. Paul's so that he could hear the bell ring before he returned to England.

In March 1914 when the caretaker went to ready the fire for the service, he found the church filled with smoke. He rang the bell as a fire alarm but as it was nearly time for the service, no one realized there was a fire. The fire destroyed the church.

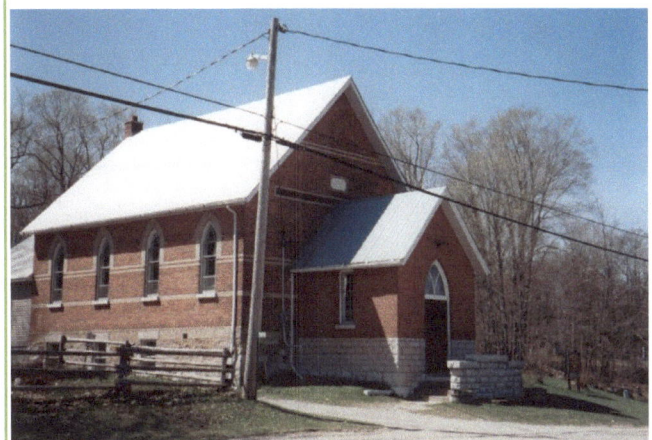

Sebright, Ramara Township
Sebright United
April 21, 1898

Severn Falls, Severn Township
Severn Falls Protestant Chapel
August 1999

Shanty Bay, Oro-Medonte Township
St. Thomas Anglican
May 2010

Built in 1838, the walls of this church are made of clay mixed with straw (preferably barley straw). Each three foot block was made and left to dry and settle before the next block was added. This type of wall provides good insulation and is long wearing as long as there is no dampness allowed to enter. The church is still in active use.

Singhampton, Clearview Township
St. Paul's Anglican
August 11, 2006

Stayner, Clearview Township
Brethren in Christ (former)
May 17, 2000

To elect a minister, ballots were used. When there were three candidates with the same number of votes, they used three pieces of paper with a name on each. The papers were dropped to the floor. If only one landed face up, that name would become the minister. If two were face up, the third name would be eliminated and one paper with a name on either side was dropped. The name that faced up became the minister.

This church is across the road from the current church building.

Stayner, Clearview Township
Brethren in Christ
August 1999

Stayner, Clearview Township
Centennial United
November 2001

Stayner, Clearview Township
Church of the Good Shepherd Anglican
September 7, 1997

Stayner, Clearview Township
Clearview Community Pentecostal
December 15, 1998

Stayner, Clearview Township
Evangelical Missionary
December 5, 1998

Stayner, Clearview Township
Evangelical Missionary
Rebuilt after a fire in 2009.

S

We Worship the Lord in Simcoe County Churches | 73

Stayner, Clearview Township
First Baptist
December 15, 1998

Stayner, Clearview Township
Jubilee Presbyterian
September 5, 1997

The first Presbyterian church in Stayner was built in 1862.

The Jubilee Presbyterian church was built in 1888, the Golden Jubilee year of the reign of Queen Victoria. An addition was built in 1978 when Queen Elizabeth II celebrated her 25th Jubilee.

Stayner, Clearview Township
St. Patrick's Roman Catholic

Strongville, Clearview Township
Strongville Gospel Hall
August 2013

Stroud, Town of Innisfil

St. James United
October 1996

Stroud, Town of Innisfil
Stroud Presbyterian
July 2011

Sunnidale Corners, Clearview Township
Zion Presbyterian
1997

Tay Township
St. John's Anglican cairn
October 6, 2006

Thompsonville, Town of New Tecumseth
Thompsonville United cairn
May 25, 2005

When the 50th anniversary of the church was celebrated, the building was full so the windows were raised and cars parked two or three deep to hear the singing and preaching.

Thornton, Essa Township
New Life Community Christian
May 28, 2013

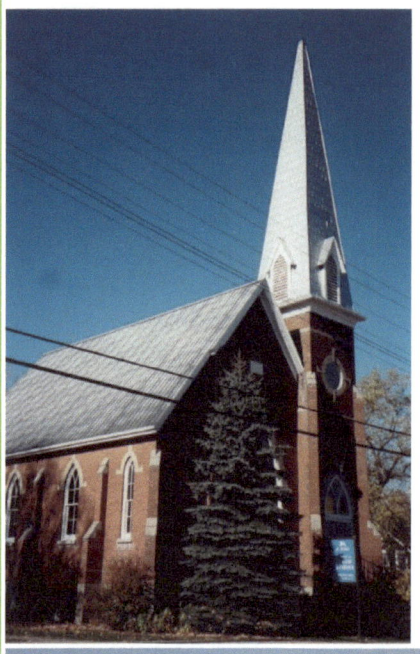

Thornton, Essa Township
Simcoe Free Church
1996

This was St. Jude's Anglican.

Thornton, Essa Township
Trinity United
1996

Thunder Beach, Tiny Township
St. Florence Roman Catholic
May 1997

Tottenham, Town of New Tecumseth
Christ Church Anglican
June 16, 1999

The pipe organ in this church was moved from St. Mark's Anglican in Orangeville by the men of the congregation. It was installed under the guidance of an organist from Alliston, Lawrence Lindsay.

Tottenham, Town of New Tecumseth
Fraser Presbyterian
September 2013
The church was first lighted by electricity in April 1891.

Tottenham, Town of New Tecumseth
Hillside Community Church
May 25, 2005

Tottenham, Town of New Tecumseth
St. Francis Xavier Roman Catholic
May 25, 2005

We Worship the Lord in Simcoe County Churches

Tottenham, Town of New Tecumseth
Tottenham United
June 16, 1999

In January 1895, fire destroyed the church and eighty other buildings in town.

A member of the congregation wrote to Andrew Carnegie (of free library building fame) to ask for financial help in buying a pipe organ for the church. Carnegie agreed to pay half and the congregation raised the other half.

Udney, Ramara Township
Udney United (former)
May 1997

Uptergrove, Ramara Township
Knox Presbyterian
April 1998

This congregation did not have a minister for twenty years between 1856 and 1876. Instead, worship was led by a member of the community, an early Scottish settler.

Uptergrove, Ramara Township
St. Columbkille's Roman Catholic
July 5, 2013

Utopia, Essa Township
St. George's Anglican
2013

Utopia, Essa Township
Utopia United (former)

Vasey, Tay Township
Unity United
May 2013

Victoria Harbour, Tay Township
St. John's United (former)
September 1999

Victoria Harbour, Tay Township
St. Mary's Roman Catholic
July 24, 2013

In 1937, a fire broke out in the home of church caretaker Hector St. Amant and quickly spread to the neighbouring church. It was totally destroyed but rebuilt that year.

Victoria Harbour, Tay Township
St. Paul's Presbyterian
July 24, 2013

Victoria Harbour, Tay Township
Victory Baptist
2013

Warminster, Oro-Medonte Township
Sacred Heart Roman Catholic
May 2010

Warminster, Oro-Medonte Township
Warminster United (former)

Wasaga Beach, Town of
Faith Missionary
February 21, 1999

Wasaga Beach, Town of
Lighthouse Community
August 2013

Wasaga Beach, Town of
Prince of Peace Anglican
November 23, 2001

Wasaga Beach, Town of
St. Noel Chabonel Roman Catholic
August 2013

Opened in 1959, this church is named for a Jesuit priest murdered by aboriginals in 1649. They threw his body into the Nottawasaga River at Wasaga Beach.

Wasaga Beach, Town of
Wasaga Christian
August 2013

Wasaga Beach, Town of
Wasaga Beach Community Presbyterian
February 21, 1999

Wasaga Beach, Town of
Wasaga Beach United
August 2013

Washago, Severn Township
Heritage United
May 1997

This was built as a Presbyterian church in 1874. The Governor General of Canada, Lord Dufferin, laid the cornerstone.

Washago, Severn Township
St. Francis of Assisi Roman Catholic
July 23, 2002

Washago, Severn Township
St. Paul's Anglican
June 1, 2006

Waubaushene, Tay Township
Christ Church Anglican
2011

When 109 years old, this church was carefully lifted and a new basement dug beneath. The interior is lined with ash wood that is said to be knot free.

Waubaushene, Tay Township
Gospel Hall
September 1999

Waubaushene, Tay Township
St. John's Roman Catholic (former)
June 6, 2004

When this new church was dedicated in 1870, the owner of Waubaushene Mills sent his steamer to Penetanguishene to carry people to the service free of charge. He donated the land and some of the lumber for the building.

Waubaushene, Tay Township
St. John's Roman Catholic

Waverley, Tay Township
Gospel Hall
March 16, 1998

Waverley, Tay Township
St. John's Anglican
June 2009

Waverley, Tay Township
Waverley United

Woodland Beach, Springwater Township
Woodland Beach Community Church

Wyebridge, Tiny Township
Church of the Good Shepherd Anglican
May 1997

Wyebridge, Tiny Township
St. Andrew's Presbyterian (former)
June 6, 2009
The church opened September 28, 1890.

Wyevale, Tiny Township
Wyevale Free Methodist
May 2009

Wyevale, Tiny Township
Wyevale United
2009

In Closing

Beautiful is the large church
With stately arch and steeple

Neighbourly is the small church
With groups of friendly people

Reverent is the old church
With centuries of grace

And a wooden church or stone church
Can hold an altar place

And whether it be a rich church
Or a poor church anywhere

Truly it is a *great* church
If God is worshipped there!

www.ingramcontent.com/pod-product-compliance
Lightning Source LLC
Chambersburg PA
CBHW042018150426
43197CB00002B/64